Century
12.50

THE HOUND OF HEAVEN

THE HOUND OF HEAVEN

FRANCIS THOMPSON

BIOGRAPHICAL SKETCH AND NOTES BY
MICHAEL A. KELLY, C. S. Sp.
INTRODUCTION BY
KATHERINE BRÉGY

PETER REILLY, PUBLISHER
PHILADELPHIA
1916

CONTENTS

BIBLIOGRAPHY

POEMS .... *John Lane Company*

SISTER SONGS .... *John Lane Company*

NEW POEMS .... *John Lane Company*

THE HOUND OF HEAVEN .... *Burns and Oates*

SELECTED POEMS, with biographical note by Wilfrid Meynell .... *John Lane Company*

HEALTH AND HOLINESS .... *Herder*

SHELLEY, with an introduction by the Right Hon. George Wyndham ...... *John Lane Company*

ST. IGNATIUS LOYOLA .... *Burns and Oates*

LIFE AND LABOURS OF ST. JOHN BAPTIST DE LA SALLE .... *Herder*

WORKS, three volumes .... *Charles Scribner's Sons*

LIFE, By Everard Meynell. *Charles Scribner's Sons*

FRANCIS THOMPSON, the Preston-born poet, by John Thompson .... *Herder*

INTRODUCTION

INTRODUCTION

THERE is scarcely another religious poem in our language which one would dare to cite before the dual, and very different, bars of theology and rhetoric as the editor has here cited the *Hound of Heaven.* Indeed, there are very few religious poems in any language which would stand that exacting test. I remember, as a schoolgirl, having to analyse, line by line and word by word, the entire structure of *As You Like It.* It seemed like stretching a fairy upon the dissecting table! No doubt I learned several things from the experiment; but I am certain my most lasting discovery was that Shakespeare's comedy remained beautiful and blithe and alive in spite of the worst that schoolrooms could do to it.

This is the supreme test of greatness—that it shall stand all tests: just as it is the supreme test of friendship when we cannot know our friends too well. And by this test one feels that the present attempt has been more than justified. If to instruct one soul in Christian faith is to cover a multitude of sins, surely to open even one growing mind, even one unfolding heart, to the beauties of Christian poetry is no small thing. The Rev. Frederick William Faber pointed out long ago that a taste for reading, rightly directed, was perhaps the greatest of all natural aids to spiritual growth.

All the world knows now that Francis Thompson was one of the supreme poets of nineteenth century England. And because of his gorgeous imagery, his unusual verse—construction, his rich diction and his profoundly mystical message, he will stand almost limitless elucidation: moreover these elucidations, these "corollaries" of his poetry, are generally far too vital to be relegated to foot-notes. This is the fertility of the annotator's field. Thompson was no believer in the much-advertised poetry of everyday speech. While detesting literary affectations, he declared once that "To write plainly on a fine subject is to set a jewel in wood." Hence we find him constantly dropping into sonorous Latinisms, or reviving the forgotten splendors of Elizabethan English, or dauntlessly coining new words for himself. His biographer Mr. Everard Meynell, tells us the poet took a half-mischievous interest in watching such expressions of his own ('rumorous', 'roseal,' 'labyrinthine' were some of them), gradually slip into contemporary literature; and wonders what he might have thought to hear, some two years after his death, many of these very words used in the rostrum of English politics.

All this is very curious and instructive. Yet who, in reading the present volume, can fail to feel that the value of its notes lies less in their explanation of metre or reference than in their flashes of human and even superhuman insight? Such, for instance, is the simple observation that the title of Thompson's poem may seem out of place to those unfamiliar with its matter, or to "*anyone who has never felt the pursuit of God's love.*" No man can explain a great work of art in mere terms of black and white: and so at their best these "notes" are not notes at all, but rather meditations. Surely by that name must we call the searching and comforting comment upon lines 19–20: "*The Great Temptation;*" and *àpropos* of line 114, his remark that "we are all Pelagians at heart, and would wish to be able to work out our salvation without God's grace!" Again, it is very illuminating to find in the patient, profound judgment that is by right the priest's—but never by any chance the world's!—Oscar Wilde's discovery that God's love is "eternally given to that which is eternally unworthy" linked with St. Paul's words to the Corinthians on one side, and on the other with Thompson's insistent message to modern England.

The Hound of Heaven is not merely a great piece of literature, nor in Coventry Patmore's words "one of the very few great odes" in the English language: it is also a great page of soul autobiography. It is universal because it is so sincerely personal. And, granting that our tongue endures, there seems every reason to believe that men will read this poem as long as they continue to read the

Confessions of St. Augustin,—and for much the same reason! Perhaps because of Francis Thompson's unhidden frailties, one has the less hesitation in laying hold upon his strength. And surely it is not alone the *Hound,* but every page of his work and even the record of his troublous life, which proves strength to have been the *truest* part: the part, that is, which Francis himself *loved* and *willed.* He fought from the first against great odds. Often, by men's poor judgment, he seemed to fail. But he never betrayed nor ever weakly temporised his Vision of the Ideal.

Those who have made the present poem their own will pass on joyously to Thompson's other work, and will find in its variety the same costly penetration of human heart and mind and soul. "To be the poet of the return to Nature is somewhat," he once gravely wrote; "but I would be the poet of the return to God!" When all is said, that is why the *Hound of Heaven,* once a poem for the literary elect, is now to be popularised for our schools. And the star-crossed singer who delighted to walk hand-in-hand with his child-friend through poppy fields, and who had such frank predilection for "the nurseries of Heaven," would love best to have it so.

KATHERINE BREGY.

August, 1915.

LIFE OF FRANCIS THOMPSON

FRANCIS THOMPSON

1859–1907

When "In Memoriam" was given to the world it was and it still remains a puzzle to the average reader because unlike another great English poet mourning a similar sorrow the writer passes from his sorrow to himself. "Lycidas is dead," and Milton cannot get away from the fact; Hallam is dead, and his death is but the prelude of endless discussion; for behind the sobbing of the poet's soul an undercurrent of thought makes itself heard sometimes doubtful and wavering, sometimes clear and thrilling, telling the story of more than a soul in pain for the death of a friend. It is rather the story of a soul in pain for itself, searching now in the broad light of Revelation, now in the darkness of Pantheism, the solution of its own existence and the solace of its own pain. It is but another chapter in a story that is almost as old as the world and will grow old with it:

> "Into this Universe, and Why not knowing
> Nor *Whence,* like Water willy-nilly flowing;
> And out of it, as Wind along the Waste,
> I know not *Whither,* willy-nilly blowing."

Whether, however, it be expressed thus in the sad blasphemies of an Omar Khayyam, or resolve itself into the pathetic questionings of an Augustin, it is for ever and for ever but an echo of the "sad sweet music of humanity." But what was to Omar only "to-morrow's tangle," what was only a "riddle of the painful earth" to Tennyson became to St. Augustin not merely the beginning of faith, but the most cogent of realities: "Thou hast made us for Thyself, O Lord, and our heart will be for ever unrested until it rest in Thee." Side by side with this grand confession of the saint, the shadowy results of the nine years' brooding of Tennyson,—"the broken lights" of God, even if they do preserve all the glamor of poetic beauty, fail utterly as a solution of the great problem of life. It is, therefore, with grateful hearts that we turn in an age of materialism and voluntary darkness to the cry of another soul out of the depths, a cry sometimes as troubled and as bitter as that of Omar, sometimes as querulous and as pleading as that of Tennyson, but always as passionate and as final in its conclusions as that of St. Augustin.

It must nevertheless be said that the Hound of Heaven remains likewise to many an enigma. The vibrant intensity of the poet's feeling leads him frequently away from the by-paths of current human expression. Yet what so many persist in thinking exaggeration is but the record of the struggle of a soul with what, in an age like ours, when "there is no one who thinks in his heart," is also outside of the ordinary current of human feelings. If even the Book of the Psalms could *now* by some strange accident fall for the first time into the hands of some amateur literary critic, it would run the risk of, if not being laid aside in disgust, at least being catalogued as something which could find no place in the modern trend and development of thought, for unfamiliarity with any piece of writing, because it is the product either of another time than ours or of another spirit than ours furnishes too often only a reason for an easy and sympathetic dismissal of the same. The Hound of Heaven judged in this spirit has more than once been condemned as artificial and unreal. Yet to say the truth this poem is not only the masterpiece of Thompson but it stands out among all the productions of modern literature as a masterpiece in itself. A great poem in its sublime cadences and its wealth of imagery it appeals both to the ear and to the imagination; it is a great poem still more in the sense that the Psalms remain the most wonderful poetry of all time for in them the Divine Singer fingers in turn every stop of the human soul—love, pathos, ecstasy, joy, sorrow, repentance and even despair. The Hound of Heaven is indeed the revelation of a soul. But it is not the soul of a pagan already conquered by unbelief and pessimism for whom life is but

"A moment's halt—a momentary Taste
Of Being from the well amid the Waste—
And lo!—the phantom caravan has reached
The Nothing it set out from— . . . ."

Nor is it the soul of a half christian dilettante vaguely whispering to himself:

" My own dim life should teach me this,
That life shall live for evermore
Else earth is darkness at the core
And dust and ashes all that is."

But it is the soul of a christian and a man who once having felt the mysterious strength of Divine Grace is learning or has learned that for the Grace of God there can be no substitute. The mask of everyday life is off and self-confessed the man stands before us with his very heart laid bare,—

" Whom wilt thou find to love ignoble thee
Save Me, save only Me? "

That this was or was not the object of Francis Thompson when he penned the Hound of Heaven cannot be said with certainty, but he certainly must have thought and felt what he wrote, else it would never have been written. It is, consequently, apart almost from the glowing language in which thought and feeling have here found expression, this intensely human element in the poem which is the foundation of the universality of its appeal and of the immortality of its message. Because, if the truth were known, it is the touch of grace, far more than the touch of nature, that makes the whole world kin. And thus while there exists nowadays a certain well-defined tendency to confound mysticism with the half-sentimental, half-philosophical vaporings of would-be poets of humanity, a tendency to make God and religion things as nebulous as their idle dreams, Francis Thompson goes his way alone, occupies a position unique, apart,—he is for and from all time; and his poem is one of the highest and sweetest expressions of the " true light which enlighteneth every man that cometh into the world," that light that shines forever in the darkness and which the darkness fails so frequently to comprehend.

Francis Thompson was born in the town of Preston, Lancashire, England, nine days before Christmas in the year 1859. His father was Charles Thompson, a physician, and his mother, a convert to Catholicism, was, by maiden name, Mary Morton. He was the second of a family of five children, of whom only two survived him. His childhood was not unhappy,—his mother and his sisters, books and toys dividing almost equally his attention, and he went, in later years, back frequently to it in spirit. At the age of eleven Ushaw College received him as one of its pupils, and for seven years under the nickname of " Tommy," he, " a shy and unusual boy," came into contact with the usual ups and downs of English school-boy life. In those days, it is related, he was a great reader of books as well as of school-books. Destined as he had been, in the minds of his parents, for the priesthood, it was found that his native indolence and indifference due more to lack perhaps of physical health than of anything else barred him from such a vocation, and it was these same faults of character which spoiled the next six years of his life spent as a medical student at Owen's College, Manchester. He, while there, studied medicine far less than he read poetry, and it is probably to his natural predisposition to idleness, closing to him the career of either doctor or divine, that we are indebted for Francis Thompson and the Hound of Heaven. He failed, one might say "conscientiously," in each of his successive examinations for medicine, to the despair of his father who, having tried his son at one or two minor business ventures calling for less energy and application than a professional career, told him plainly at length that "if he could find no other means of support, the only career open to him was to enlist as a soldier." And a soldier he would have been, the last resource of many a *carrière manquée,* had he been physically fit.

This natural unfitness for the practical issues of life by which Thompson was so much handicapped when other young men of his age were hewing their way with healthy strokes into the heart of worldly success left him friendless and homeless and proved for him the source of countless miseries. London, the Mecca of all Englishmen, which holds in its heart far from the noise and bustle of the world a sanctuary for its men of genius, cast its spell upon Thompson also and beckoned him from his home. But

London so kind to its dead poets was unkind to Thompson living. Homeless at home, he fared no better in London, for, having carried with him his shyness and his lack of physical health what wonder if he sank into insignificance and forgetfulness among the blatant thoroughfares and the robust life of the city. He has preserved for us a record of at least one strange kindness done him in his darkest hour of need. But, another who befriended him (as he befriended others) in giving him work to do, (a certain Mr. McMaster), was compelled to say of him: "Thompson was my only failure." And although he does refer to a certain habit of prayer by Thompson, he hints openly that the latter had at that time fallen away from the practices of the Catholic faith. Indeed, it would seem that Francis Thompson's religion, nominally Catholic, was consciously or unconsciously of the type of Catholicism that cannot be found in churches. "He loved" nevertheless "the beauty of the house of God," and no poet perhaps ever divined as well the mystical meaning of the pomp of the Church's liturgy. A holiday at home which left him more shiftless than ever was followed by his dismissal from the workshop of his benefactor. What he suffered then, eking out an existence as a shoe-black, as a seller of matches, as a cab-caller in the streets of London, is best known only to himself, but the suffering with all its attendant horrors, it cannot be denied was of his own choosing and making. Of all the circumstances that contributed to his misery the greatest was himself. . . . . . . It was, however, only as a Gethsemani, a darkness before the dawn, and from it at length, he too

> ". . . . . rose and past
> Bearing a lifelong hunger in his heart"—

a hunger for God. Because from the memory of those very days, beautiful as a rose blooming upon a grave, came, fragrant with repentance, and with hope, radiant with light and color a masterpiece of song. The Hound of Heaven tells of a heart that is still bleeding from the struggle but which bleeds no longer in vain; it is the rose of the tombs yielding its perfume.

The light and strength came to Thompson, it might be said, from the date of the publication in Merrie England (a review edited by Mr. Wilfrid Meynell, and dedicated to criticism literary as well as artistic) of an article of his called "Paganism—Old and New." Thompson had looked for a publisher only, and found instead a friend and a family of friends. Little by little, his shattered body was restored to a minimum of health and his poor soul was freed from its loneliness. Yet the crisis through which he had passed left him for the remainder of his days always vacillating and hesitating, intensified his disposition to laziness, and marked him out as a model of unpunctuality. It is from this date (1888) that he began to take his place in literature, the "Ode to the Setting Sun" having been published about this time. One of the most wonderful essays of modern times,—his essay on Shelley, was rejected by the Dublin Review and did not appear until twenty years later, after the poet's death, to be acclaimed at that late date as the "most important contribution made to English Literature for twenty years." "Sister Songs" began to take shape, and the Hound of Heaven was written in 1891 (published, however, only in 1895). A book-notice of Thompson's on General Booth's "Darkest England" poignant with bitter memories of his own darkness when under the "bashless inquisition of each star," he had himself

> "Suffered the trampling hoof of every hour
> In night's slow-wheeléd car,"

brought to Thompson the notice of Cardinal Manning, and the unqualified approbation of Mr. W. T. Stead then enjoying his world-wide reputation as a journalist and editor of the "Review of Reviews." The year 1892 saw Manning in his grave and Thompson wrote his lines "To the Dead Cardinal of Westminster."

For some time Francis Thompson was on the journalistic staff of the Weekly Register (another paper of Mr. Meynell's) but he was, as often as not, a disappointing contributor, failing repeatedly to be in time with his "copy." In 1892 he betook himself to the Franciscan Monastery at Pantasaph, in Wales, where, already Franciscan in simplicity and in name, he found himself very much at home. He moved later to a cottage hard by; and the influence of association with learned and pious men of God, his long walks in the country and the open air, together with the wholesome silence of the place, accomplished a wonderful change in the poet, and brought about in a great measure what the sympathy of Mr. Meynell had already begun, for, thenceforward, although bodily health was never his to any very marked degree, he began to be remembered by his friends for a laugh as graceful and as lighthearted as any child's. The Meynell family, to whose kindness and sympathy, based on a perfect understanding of one who never, perhaps, understood himself, every reader and lover of Thompson is almost as much indebted as was the Poet himself, will go down in the history of letters not only as a family richly endowed with the genius which we call literature, but, if it were possible, more richly endowed with the genius which we call appreciation. And, perhaps, had his father understood the seeming waywardness of Francis as a student but half as well as his friends did his shabbiness and his shiftlessness of later years no one would ever have had to deplore or to excuse his mistakes. To the eternal credit of Francis Thompson it must be said that he responded fully to their sympathy and never once betrayed their trust; and if it be true that all things are done on earth as well as in heaven by love, the truth has been once more exemplified in the remodelling and remaking of the life of Francis Thompson. It was during this stay at

Pantasaph that the poet's father died without seeing him, and that Thompson met Coventry Patmore for the first time. Nothing could exceed Patmore's graceful friendliness to his coming brother-poet; and when Patmore died in 1896, Thompson feeling his death very acutely went back to London, where, during the closing years of his own life, mainly through the kindness of the Meynells, he made the acquaintance of most of the literary celebrities of the time.

For several years Thompson worked steadily and unsteadily at reviewing and journalism under one form or another on the staff now of the Academy, now of the Athenaeum, now of other periodicals. But the work by which he is best remembered was already done. His letters about this time are many and beautiful, beautiful just as much in what he wrote in them by way of digression as in what he would expressly wish to write. His pocket and his wardrobe were in constant danger of being empty, but neither the emptiness of his pocket nor the scantiness of his wardrobe had further effect on him than to occasion sometimes a childlike impatience. The comparison of his poverty to that of St. Francis of Assisi, although ingenious and sympathetic, has, however, but one main foundation, namely, poverty! They were both poor; but Francis Bernardone was poor by set choice and purpose, while Francis Thompson was poor by accident and indolence. Poverty to the one was the basis of a divine life, to the other it was but a helpless condition of existence. To say, nevertheless, that they had nothing in common, would be wrong; both arrived at the same point, detachment, but through ways as differing and different as prodigality differs from charity.

Francis Thompson's health, never of the robust type, was frequently to him a source of preoccupation; and the battling of this poor soul, so little fitted for the practical things of life, against the exigencies of money matters did not now ameliorate his condition. Little by little he failed visibly. Despondent days and dark hours hurried him likewise to the end. His Franciscan friends never forgot him and invited him to rest with them. But the hand of the dreadful disease, Consumption, was at his throat, and neither care nor kindness, both of which were lavished upon him, first by Mr. Blunt at his place in Sussex, afterwards by Sister Michael at the Hospital of St. John and St. Elizabeth, could lengthen his sojourn upon earth. Death came to him on November 13, 1907, and his body was laid to rest in St. Mary's Cemetery, Kensal Green. Never of any one man perhaps were the words of Gray's epitaph more true: "He gave to misery (all he had) a tear,"—it was the Hound of Heaven,—"He gained from heaven ('twas all he wished) a friend," and the friend was Mr. Wilfrid Meynell.

M. A. K.

Cape May Point,
August 15, 1915.

THE HOUND OF HEAVEN

THE HOUND OF HEAVEN

By Francis Thompson

I fled Him, down the nights and down the days;
  I fled Him, down the arches of the years;
I fled Him, down the labyrinthine ways
  Of my own mind; and in the mist of tears
I hid from Him, and under running laughter.
          Up vistaed hopes, I sped;
          And shot, precipitated,
Adown Titanic glooms of chasmèd fears,
  From those strong Feet that followed, followed after.
          But with unhurrying chase,
          And unperturbèd pace,
    Deliberate speed, majestic instancy,
          They beat—and a Voice beat
          More instant than the Feet—
    "All things betray thee, who betrayest Me."

          I pleaded, outlaw-wise,
By many a hearted casement, curtained red,
    Trellised with intertwining charities;

(For, though I knew His love Who followed,
Yet was I sore adread
Lest, having Him, I must have naught beside)
But, if one little casement parted wide,
The gust of His approach would clash it to.
Fear wist not to evade as Love wist to pursue.
Across the margent of the world I fled,
And troubled the gold gateways of the stars,
Smiting for shelter on their clangèd bars;
Fretted to dulcet jars
And silvern chatter the pale ports o' the moon.
I said to dawn: Be sudden; to eve: Be soon—
With thy young skyey blossoms heap me over
From this tremendous Lover!
Float thy vague veil about me, lest He see!
I tempted all His servitors, but to find
My own betrayal in their constancy,
In faith to Him their fickleness to me,
Their traitorous trueness, and their loyal deceit.
To all swift things for swiftness did I sue;
Clung to the whistling mane of every wind.
But whether they swept, smoothly fleet,
The long savannahs of the blue;
Or whether, Thunder-driven,

They clanged His chariot 'thwart a heaven,
Plashy with flying lightnings round the spurn o'
their feet:—
Fear wist not to evade as Love wist to pursue.
Still with unhurrying chase,
And unperturbèd pace,
Deliberate speed, majestic instancy,
Came on the following Feet,
And a Voice above their beat—
"Naught shelters thee, who wilt not shelter
Me."

I sought no more that, after which I strayed,
In face of man or maid;
But still within the little children's eyes
Seems something, something that replies,
They, at least, are for me, surely for me!
I turned me to them very wistfully;
But just as their young eyes grew sudden fair
With dawning answers there,
Their angel plucked them from me by the hair.
"Come then, ye other children, Nature's—share
With me" (said I) "your delicate fellow-
ship;

Let me greet you lip to lip,
Let me twine with you caresses,
Wantoning
With our Lady-Mother's vagrant tresses,
Banqueting
With her in her wind-walled palace,
Underneath her azured daïs,
Quaffing, as your taintless way is,
From a chalice
Lucent-weeping out of the dayspring."
So it was done:
I, in their delicate fellowship was one—
Drew the bolt of Nature's secrecies.
I knew all the swift importings
On the wilful face of skies;
I knew how the clouds arise,
Spumèd of the wild sea-snortings;
All that's born or dies
Rose and drooped with; made them shapers
Of mine own moods, or wailful or divine—
With them joyed and was bereaven.
I was heavy with the even,
When she lit her glimmering tapers
Round the day's dead sanctities.

I laughed in the morning's eyes.
I triumphed and I saddened with all weather,
Heaven and I wept together,
And its sweet tears were salt with mortal mine;
Against the red throb of its sunset-heart
I laid my own to beat,
And share commingling heat;
But not by that, by that, was eased my human smart.
In vain my tears were wet on Heaven's grey cheek.
For ah! we know not what each other says,
These things and I; in sound *I* speak—
Their sound is but their stir, they speak in silences.
Nature, poor stepdame, cannot slake my drought;
Let her, if she would owe me,
Drop yon blue bosom-veil of sky, and show me
The breasts o' her tenderness:
Never did any milk of hers once bless
My thirsting mouth.
Nigh and nigh, draws the chase,
With unperturbèd pace,
Deliberate speed, majestic instancy,
And past those noisèd Feet

A Voice comes yet more fleet—
"Lo! naught contents thee, who content'st not Me."

Naked I wait Thy love's uplifted stroke!
My harness piece by piece Thou hast hewn from me,
And smitten me to my knee;
I am defenceless utterly.
I slept, methinks, and woke,
And, slowly gazing, find me stripped in sleep.
In the rash lustihead of my young powers,
I shook the pillaring hours
And pulled my life upon me; grimed with smears,
I stand amid the dust o' the mounded years—
My mangled youth lies dead beneath the heap.
My days have crackled and gone up in smoke,
Have puffed and burst as sun-starts on a stream.
Yea, faileth now even dream
The dreamer, and the lute the lutanist;
Even the linked fantasies, in whose blossomy twist
I swung the earth a trinket at my wrist,
Are yielding; cords of all too weak account
For earth, with heavy griefs so overplussed.

Ah! is Thy love indeed
A weed, albeit an amaranthine weed,
Suffering no flowers except its own to mount?
Ah! must—
Designer infinite!—
Ah! must Thou char the wood ere Thou canst limn with it?
My freshness spent its wavering shower i' the dust;
And now my heart is as a broken fount,
Wherein tear-drippings stagnate, spilt down ever
From the dank thoughts that shiver
Upon the sighful branches of my mind.
Such is; what is to be?
The pulp so bitter, how shall taste the rind?
I dimly guess what Time in mists confounds;
Yet ever and anon a trumpet sounds
From the hid battlements of Eternity,
Those shaken mists a space unsettle, then
Round the half-glimpsèd turrets slowly wash again;
But not ere Him Who summoneth
I first have seen, enwound
With glooming robes purpureal, cypress-crowned;
His Name I know, and what His trumpet saith.
Whether man's heart or life it be which yields

Thee harvest, must Thy harvest fields
Be dunged with rotten death?
Now of that long pursuit
Comes on at hand the bruit;
That Voice is round me like a bursting sea:
"And is thy earth so marred,
Shattered in shard on shard?
Lo, all things fly thee, for thou fliest Me!

Strange, piteous, futile thing!
Wherefore should any set thee love apart?
Seeing none but I makes much of naught" (He said),
"And human love needs human meriting:
How hast thou merited—
Of all man's clotted clay the dingiest clot?
Alack, thou knowest not
How little worthy of any love thou art!
Whom wilt thou find to love ignoble thee,
Save Me, save only Me?
All which I took from thee I did but take,
Not for thy harms,
But just that thou might'st seek it in My arms.
All which thy child's mistake

Fancies as lost, I have stored for thee at home:
Rise, clasp My hand, and come."

Halts by me that footfall;
Is my gloom, after all,
Shade of His hand, outstretched caressingly?
"Ah, fondest, blindest, weakest,
I am He Whom thou seekest!
Thou dravest love from thee, who dravest Me."

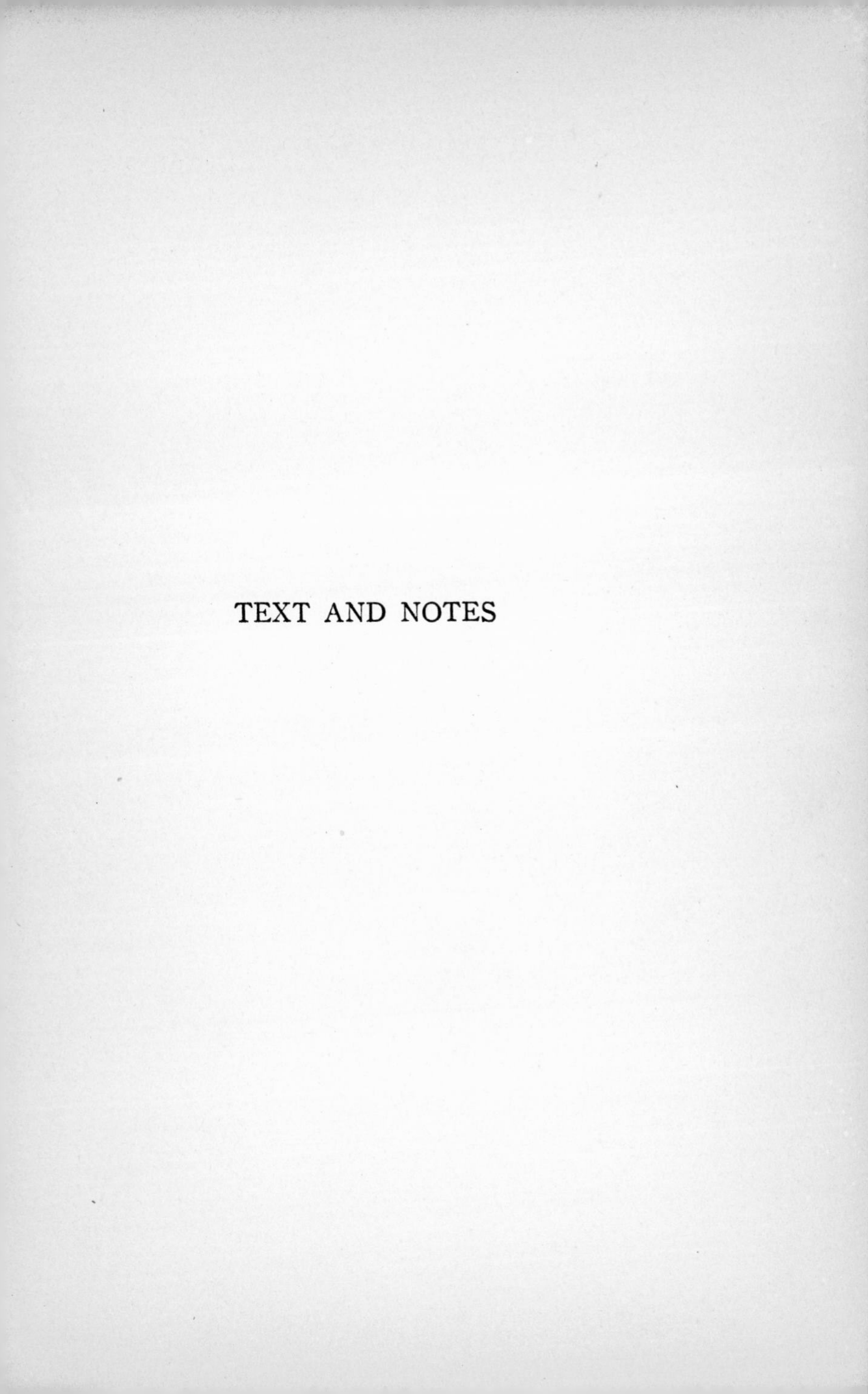

TEXT AND NOTES

TEXT AND NOTES

1–6. I fled Him, down the nights and down the days;
    I fled Him, down the arches of the years;
I fled Him down the labyrinthine ways
    Of my own mind; and in the mist of tears
I hid from Him, and under running laughter.
        Up vistaed hopes, I sped;

1 An. echo of Psalm 138. Cf. v. 7: "Whither shall I go from Thy spirit? or whither shall I flee from Thy face?"

Fled Him.—i. e., fled from Him. The expression is stronger.

Nights, days, years.—He fled from God all the time of his life.

2. **Arches.**—Addison, in his "Vision of Mirza," represents life as an immense ocean, spanned by a bridge, both ends of which are lost in the mists of eternity. The arches of this bridge are the years. Here, however, the metaphor represents rather a succession of arches or archways through which the soul flies from God.

3. **Labyrinthine ways** of the mind is a fitting expression, because we are only too often deluded by our own conceits, and "in wandering mazes lost." The word "labyrinth" means a maze. The original Labyrinth is in the Mythology (Gr.). In it was a monster—the Minotaur, half man, half bull—to whom a yearly tribute of human lives was paid. He was slain by Theseus who, by means of a silken thread held at the entrance by Ariadne, was guided back to freedom. (Ovid.) The earliest and most renowned labyrinth was, however, in Egypt, near Lake Moeris; it was half under ground, and contained 3000 apartments.

4. **Mist of tears.**—Tears, when they are like the tears of Christ—"And Jesus wept"—i. e., tears of expiation, atonement and sympathy, draw us closer to God. They are no mist; all other tears are the mist that hides us from God, and God from us. Yet Louis Veuillot says:

"For there are things our weakling eyes can never see
But through their tears." (Trans.)

5. **Running laughter.**—We say "rippling" laughter. If there are tears which hide us from God, there is, likewise, a joy—the joy that is not "in the Lord"—where God never dwells.

6. **Vistaed.**—A curious adjective, coined from the word "vista." *Vista* is the Italian word for a view. The more usual sense of the word is an open space in a wood (or a prospect through an avenue, as of trees) well-lighted in comparison with the surrounding gloom; hence ***vistaed hopes.***

7–15. And shot, precipitated,
Adown Titantic glooms of chasmèd fears,
From those strong Feet that followed, followed after.
But with unhurrying chase,
And unperturbèd pace,
Deliberate speed, majestic instancy,
They beat—and a Voice beat
More instant than the Feet—
"All things betray thee, who betrayest Me."

7–8. **Titanic.**—Titan was a name in the Greek Mythology given to any one of the six sons and six daughters of Uranus (heaven) and Gaea (earth). After having been hurled from heaven into nether darkness by Jupiter, they were assisted in their struggle with him by the hundred-handed giants. *Titanic* means, therefore, monstrous or rebellious. Fear, too, is a monster, condemned to perpetual ***glooms;*** it is, besides, the great danger, the precipice the soul must avoid in its way to God,—***chasmèd fears.*** "It is I, fear not," says the Lord.

9. **Strong Feet.**—The powerful, pursuing Feet of God, the Hound of Heaven. This name was given to God by Thompson only on account of this beautiful attribute of God, so vividly brought home to us in the Good Shepherd, namely, His pursuit of souls—swift, keen, untiring, as the greyhound after the hare. The name is new, strange, and out of place for anyone who has not read the poem, or better still, for anyone who has never felt the pursuit of God's love.

Followed.—The repetition of the word indicates the insistency of the pursuit.

10–12. Onomatopoeia. The words describe admirably the slow, undisturbed, deliberate, majestic pursuit, so worthy of a God Who is a God of strength,—of the strength that "can wait." *Unhurrying chase* is identical with *deliberate speed; and unperturbèd pace* (slow, measured tread) conveys the same idea as *majestic instancy*, and the juxtaposition of these words gives us an admirable instance, also of the figure of speech known as "oxymoron" or "paradox."

13. **They.**—The Feet of God.

Beat.—Throbbing like a pulse. The "beaten" track.

14. **Instant.**—For instantly, i. e., insistently. Latin "instare"—to press upon.

15. The whisper of God to the soul. *Betray* is a hard word. But because God is the alpha and the omega, the first and the last, everything (and it is the history of every soul) is bound to disappear from us, betray us, sooner or later, everything except God, more especially if we are false to God, and betray Him.

16–18. I pleaded, outlaw-wise,
By many a hearted casement, curtained red,
Trellised with intertwining charities;

16. **Pleaded.**—Begged for (love).

Outlaw-wise.—Like an outlaw or an outcast. John Howard Payne, author of the old ballad, "Home, Sweet Home," is said to have died, starving and homeless, within earshot of a drawing-room in which his song was being sung. Imagine his feelings, and those of our poet, hungering and homeless for love. Leaving himself, Thompson seeks (in lines 16, 17 and 18) to hide himself from heavenly love in the loves of the earth. Later, (in line 52) he shall be obliged to relinquish them.

17. **Casement.**—A poetic word for window; cf. Keats (Ode To a Nightingale):

> "Perhaps this self-same song....................
> ....hath
> Charmed magic casements, opening on the foam
> Of perilous seas, in faery lands forlorn."

Hearted, curtained red.—Both indicate the ruddy glow of love, and have reference undoubtedly to lovers' scenes at windows, many of which are classical; cf. Shakespeare (Romeo and Juliet); Tennyson (Maud); serenades.

18. **Trellised.**—Agrees with *casement*, like *hearted* and *curtained red*, and, like them, partakes of the transferred epithet inasmuch as the window was only the scene of the protestations of love. *Trellised*—adorned with trellises,—a sort of crisscross woodwork. The word as it is used here, however, presumably refers to the protestations of love crossing and recrossing like trellis-work.

Intertwining.—Like vines or ivies. This word bears out the idea conveyed in *trellised*.

Charities.—Charity is a higher name for love, but has come to mean anything done through charity, i. e., for the love of God, such as an alms given to the poor.

19–23. For, though I knew His love Who followéd,
Yet was I sore adread
Lest, having Him, I must have naught beside,
But, if one little casement parted wide,
The gust of His approach would clash it to.

19–21. **THIS IS THE GREAT TEMPTATION.**—The fear that, if we love God as God deserves to be loved, we can or could love no one else. But,—our love can be of two kinds, either admitting no increase or degree, (i.e., to love above all else in reality) or simply affective, (i. e., being solely in the affections, and consequently, admitting increase or decrease). In other words, our love may be purely spiritual, residing in the soul, and ruled by the reason, or it may be, as it is, alas, too often, when its object is what we can see and feel, in the heart alone. Pascal, in his "Pensées," has made the distinction beautifully: "Le coeur a ses raisons que la raison ne connaît pas"—"the heart has reasons the reason knows nothing of," i. e., reasons for loving. The love we should have for God is, of course, like all our loves, usually in the heart also, but not necessarily. It suffices to love Him with our reason, that is, to have the disposition never to offend Him by mortal sin. To fear loving God above all, "least we should have naught beside" bears with it its own punishment, for it causes us to love nothing at all; not God, for fear we may have no other love, and not man, for fear of offending God; and the punishment is loneliness for time and for eternity.

19. **His love.**—The great love of God for us, which satisfies the soul completely.

Who—has for antecedent "*His*"—i. e., "of Him."

20. **Adread.**—Afraid, dreading or adreading. Cf. afishing, awalking: the prefix "a" denotes continuity of action.

21. **Naught.**—Nothing. For aught (anything) and naught (nothing), the Lancashire people where Thompson was born say commonly "owt" and "nowt."

22–23. This poem is full of sobs, and these lines are one of them. The metaphor is easy to understand for anyone who has ever wished to give his heart to God, the windows just opening and disclosing the smiles and blushes of the loves of the earth, closed with a bang by the gust of God's approach. It sufficed only to hear the approach of God to have the love just born die out. The cause of this is, however, usually indirect apparently, but it is always a movement of God's grace: "My son, give *Me* thy heart!" Often, it is the constancy of the creature to God—the creature that would be beloved and finds it cannot, it must not, for God has called it, too. (See lines 34–37).

24–33. Fear wist not to evade as Love wist to pursue.
Across the margent of the world I fled,
And troubled the gold gateways of the stars,
Smiting for shelter on their clangéd bars;
Fretted to dulcet jars
And silvern chatter the pale ports o' the moon.
I said to dawn: Be sudden; to eve: Be soon—
With thy young skyey blossoms heap me over
From this tremendous lover!
Float thy vague veil about me, lest He see!

24. Fear trying to escape was powerless, or at least, less powerful than God's love pursuing.

Wist.—Old English, "witan"—to know. We say: "to wit" (meaning "for example"), to "lose one's wits." Cf. Mark ix. 6 (Protestant Bible) "For he wist not what to say," and the German proverb, "Ohne, Wissen, Ohne Sunde,"—"Where there is no knowledge there is no sin."

Evade.—Avoid, escape. Latin, "vado"—I go.

25–33. Change of scene from earth to heaven, but it is not yet the heaven of God and of His Saints. The passage is obscure. He seeks to hide himself from God amid the "Harmony of the Spheres."

Margent—is archaic for margin, marge, edge, border.

26. **Troubled.**—With repeated knockings, like the man in the Gospel who was knocking for bread, not shelter.

Gold gateways of the stars.—The outposts of heaven. The stars have a fascination for even the most restless minds. This metaphor of the *gateway of the stars* as the outposts of heaven may be said to have an echo in Campbell's "The sentinel stars set their watch in the sky," (Soldier's Dream), and Bret Harte, speaking of a star falling and going out of the sky, says that when he saw it he thought that "God somewhere had relieved a picket," (Relieving Guard). Nature, in all its forms, is a real gateway to God—"The heavens shew forth the glory of God and the firmament declareth the work of His Hands." (Psalm xviii).

27. **Smiting.**—Beating heavily and repeatedly.

Clanged.—The golden bars of the gateways ring, rattle and clang when he hammers upon them to open and yield him shelter.

28. **Fretted.**—Bears out the idea of discord contained in *dulcet jars*. To fret means to worry. Fretwork is any work (usually in wood or iron) which has the appearance of being jagged or irregular, yet on the whole symmetrical.

Dulcet.—Sweet,—old French, "doulce."

Jars.—Expresses any harsh sound or feeling that grates on the nerves. Italian, "garrire"—to rebuke. Cf. French, "guerre"—war, and Anglo-Saxon, "Yrre"—angry. Verb 'to jar' is used in the sense of "to quarrel" or "to wrangle," or even "to vibrate regularly as a pendulum," (Shakespeare).

29. **Silvern.**—Made of silver, or silvery (as of silver).

Chatter.—Idle talk, prattle, noise made by magpies, i. e., meaningless, brainless; cf. Tennyson (The Brook):

"I chatter, chatter, as I flow
To join the brimming river."

Silvern chatter.—Silver bells have a distinctly musical sound, and perhaps this is the idea the poet had in mind. The word "jar" is used as of bells ringing together. He rings the bells at the doors of the skies.

Pale ports o' the moon.—We say the "silver" moon, as well as the "pale" moon. Cf. Mrs. Caroline Norton (Bingen on the Rhine): "The . . . moon rose . . . her pale light seemed to shine." *Ports* is for portals, gateways, *O'* for "of" is archaic and colloquial. Cf. "jack o' lantern," "what o'clock is it."

30. Another echo of Psalm 138. Cf. vv. 11, 12: "And I said, 'Perhaps darkness shall cover me; and night shall be

my light in my pleasures. But darkness shall not be dark to thee, and night shall be as light as day: the darkness thereof, and the light thereof are alike (to Thee).'" Neither the dawn nor the evening can, therefore, hide him from God. When it is night, he longs for the day to come to do it, and in the day he sighs for the night. It is this persistent Presence of God, of the God from Whom he is fleeing, which gives the great pathos to the poem.

31. Addressed to the evening. The *skyey blossoms* are the stars. Cf. Longfellow (Evangeline) "Blossomed the lovely stars, the forget-me-nots of the angels."

Heap me over.—To hide him from God.

32. **Tremendous Lover.**—Oxymoron. Cf. Horace: "Splendide mendax"—magnificently false, (spoken of Hypermnestra, who deceived her father in not killing her husband as he commanded). God is, indeed, a *tremendous Lover*,—this is an expression which will live.

33. **Vague veil.**—Of darkness. (Possibly clouds, also). Cf. Longfellow (Hymn to the Night):

"I heard the trailing garments of the Night
Sweep through her marble halls!"

Lest He see.—A sob!

34–45. I tempted all His servitors, but to find
My own betrayal in their constancy,
In faith to Him their fickleness to me,
Their traitorous trueness, and their loyal deceit,
To all swift things for swiftness did I sue;
Clung to the whistling mane of every wind.
But whether they swept, smoothly fleet,
The long savannahs of the blue;
Or whether, Thunder-driven,
They clanged His chariot 'thwart a heaven,
Plashy with flying lightnings round the spurn o' their feet:—
Fear wist not to evade as Love wist to pursue.

34–37. More than one man has been brought to God by

the constancy (to God) of those he loves. They would not be tempted, because no one can serve *fully* and *perfectly* two masters. Our betrayal, our fickleness, our treachery, our deceit—no matter how they look or may be criticised,—to creatures, are or should be the measure of our constancy, our faith, our trueness, our loyalty to God. Tauler, the great German divine, was asked when did he find God, and he promptly replied: "When I left creatures." These lines are also an example of oxymoron or paradox—*traitorous trueness*, etc., a figure of speech common enough. Cf. Tennyson (Elaine—Idylls of the King):

> " .... but now
> The shackles of an old love straightened him,
> His honor rooted in dishonor stood,
> And faith unfaithful kept him falsely true."

38–44. He seeks shelter from, or forgetfulness of God in the whirl of the winds of heaven, making appeal to their swiftness,—the mad hope, nowadays, to stifle the voice of conscience, to kill the pulsations of the Holy Ghost in the excitement of the world. In those lines we have the whistle, the sweep, and the howl of the storm very aptly described by the words. This is called "onomatopoeia." In his "Essay on Criticism," Pope describes onomatopoeia thus:

> "'T is not enough no harshness gives offense,
> The sound must seem an Echo to the sense:
> Soft is the strain when Zephyr gently blows,
> And the smooth stream in smoother numbers flows;
> But when loud surges lash the sounding shore,
> The hoarse, rough verse should like the torrent roar;
> When Ajax strives some rock's vast weight to throw,
> The line, too, labors, and the words move slow,
> Not so, when swift Camilla scours the plain,
> Flies o'er th' unbending corn, and skims along the main."

In line 39, it is the whistle, in 40 and 41, it is the sweep, in 42–44, it is the full rage and howl of the storm.

38. **Sue.**—Appeal to, pursue. Cf. French, "suivre"—to follow.

39. **Mane.**—As of a horse or lion in flight—it is a pretty figure: wind-horses.

40. The alliteration in *swept* and *smoothly* echoes the sense.

41. **Savannahs.**—Spelled also "savanna." (Spanish, "Sabana"). A long, low, open plain or meadow, a prairie, covered with tall grasses. The effect of the breezes over cornfields is classical, and "*savannahs of the blue*" is such a sweet expression for the limitless skies!

42. **Thunder-driven.**—A word full of power. It is the howl of the storm.

43. **Clanged.**—A strange word here, referring to the clash of the storms. We can imagine the chariot buffeted by them, although *clanged* is active voice.

Chariot.—God riding in the winds. Pope (Essay on Man) speaks of the savage

> "................Whose untutored mind
> Sees God in clouds, and hears Him in the wind."

'Thwart.—Athwart or across. Contains the idea of impeding free progress. Tennyson (Palace of Art) uses "rock-thwarted" of waves:

> "And roar rock-thwarted under bellowing caves."

44. **Plashy.**—Literally, watery. Agrees with *heaven.* The idea is very beautiful: we can see the lightnings splashed and scattered by the wheels and the hooves of the horses like water on the streets on a very wet day. Goldsmith (Deserted Village) speaks of the "plashy spring" where the water-cress is gathered. Also cf. Milton: "He filled up unsound and plashy fens."

Flying lightnings.—Splashed from the wheels.

Spurn o' their feet.—A classical form of expression of great beauty, used here for spurning feet.

45. This line closes up the new attempt to escape God, for no matter how the wind blew, Love was stronger than fear.

46–60. Still with unhurrying chase,
And unperturbèd pace,
Deliberate speed, majestic instancy,
Came on the following Feet,
And a Voice above their beat—
"Naught shelters thee, who wilt not shelter
Me."

I sought no more that after which I strayed
In face of man or maid;
But still within the little children's eyes
Seems something, something that replies,
They, at least, are for me, surely for me!
I turned me to them very wistfully;
But just as their young eyes grew sudden fair
With dawning answers there,
Their angel plucked them from me by the hair.

46–50. The recurrence of these wonderful lines admirably bears out the idea of the poem, besides giving it a most artistic effect, like a 'motif' constantly recurring in some grand piece of music. Longfellow, in "King Robert of Sicily," notes the effect also in the chant of the "Magnificat." The proud king hears constantly recurring like a "burden or refrain," like "the throbbing of a single string," the words:

"He has put down the mighty from their seat,
And has exalted them of low degree."

50. The Voice beat more insistently before; now, it is *above* the Feet. God is gaining on the fugitive.

51. Shelters.—This is the second whisper of God, and it is full of pity. *Betray* was hard.

52–60. The scene changes again. He thinks the love of children would make him happy, and so enable him to forget God.

52–53. This is the great step towards FINDING GOD!

Father Faber says that God loves to come to lonely hearts, to hearts that have broken with everyone, even the grave of father and mother, adding that God so often knocks at the door of our hearts for entrance, and is denied, for "we have company," and then He goes away, not angrily but sorrowfully.

52. **That after which I strayed.**—This is a piece of self-accusation. Thompson wanted God, as we all do, but he did not know it. *Strayed* is, therefore, correct. Besides, it is the cry of the fruitless repentance of the wicked in the other world as recorded in the Book of Wisdom, ch. V, 6: "Ergo erravimus, etc."—"Therefore, we have strayed from the way of truth."

54. We all love little children, as Christ did. They are a revelation of God. God is in the artlessness of their ways, in the beauty of their eyes, and especially in the innocence of their hearts. God Himself is, in a way, as a child, in His simplicity—there is nothing complicated about Him, and that is why it is *so easy* to serve Him. ". . . and a little child shall lead them." (Isaiah xi–6). Oscar Wilde, in his "De Profundis" dates the beginning of his conversion, or of the realization of how it is possible to suffer and be happy, from the day on which they took his children away from him. In his new-found humiliation, he wrote: "The body of a child is as the body of the Lord, and I am unworthy of either." One of Longfellow's most graceful poems is called "The Children's Hour." And Tom Hood, relating his childhood experience (I remember, I remember, the house where I was born) tells how he thought the fir-tree tops touched the sky, and concludes with:

"It was a childish ignorance,
But now, 't is little joy
To know I'm farther off from Heaven
Than when I was a boy."

We all feel like that,—so true is it that "Heaven lies about us in our infancy." (Wordsworth—"Ode to Immortality").

55. **Something.**—The repetition of the word denotes vagueness of expectancy.

Replies.—i. e., to his own hopes, half-expressed.

56. **They.**—The little children. As tho' he would say: "Surely God will leave *them* to me, since 'theirs is the Kingdom of Heaven'."

57. **Me.**—Cognate accusative.

Wistfully.—Wishfully, longingly, but without any great hopes.

58. **Sudden.**—For suddenly; might qualify *grew* or *fair* with slight difference of meaning.

59. **Dawning answers.**—Expresses vagueness, as *something* in line 55.

60. This line seems to have reference to an incident related in the last chapter of the Book of Daniel, namely, how the angel of the Lord brought the Prophet Habacuc (by the hair of the head!) from Judea to Babylon with food for Daniel.

Query 1. Why should the angel pluck the children *so* away? Perhaps, to save the children. In any case, God always gives a mighty wrench to those whom He seeks to bring out of danger.

Query 2. Or does the poet merely mean to state that the suddenness of the action implies that his own delusion or illusion was as short-lived as is the innocence of children? Because, when their eyes grow *sudden fair* (and they know it) *with dawning answers there*, sin is not far away, and then it is farewell to innocence and their likeness to God, which is the secret of their charm.

It is a pity that the poet did not tell us here as much of his experiences with these children, as he did of his experiences with Nature's. It would have been beautiful. Cf. Thompson Sister Songs and other Poems.

The pathos of this incident reminds one of the words of Thomas Moore in "The Fire-Worshippers;"

"Oh! ever thus from childhood's hour,
I've seen my fondest hopes decay;
I never loved a tree or flower,
But 't was the first to fade away.
I never nursed a dear gazelle,
To glad me with its soft black eye,
But when it came to know me well,
And love me, it was sure to die!"

61–62. "Come then, ye other children, Nature's—share
With me" (said I) "your delicate fellowship! . . . ."

61. The scene changes with an invitation to Nature's children. They can never sin, and consequently, are *always* a manifestation of God. Nature's children are the air, the earth, the sea, the sky, the light, the darkness and their various changes and manifestations. Cf. Burns (Epistle to Simpson):

"O Nature! a' thy shews an' forms
To feeling, pensive hearts hae charms!—
Whether the summer kindly warms,
Wi' life an' light,
Or winter howls, in gusty storms,
The lang, dark night!"

62. Delicate.—In the sense of the French "délicat"—dainty; cf. *taintless* (line 70).

63–69. Let me greet you lip to lip,
Let me twine with you caresses,
Wantoning
With our Lady-Mother's vagrant tresses,
Banqueting
With her in her wind-walled palace,
Underneath her azured dais,

63–64. Marks of the greatest intimacy,—kisses and caresses.

Greet.—To salute or welcome. Cf. St. Paul (I Cor. xvi–20) : " Greet one another with a holy kiss."

Twine.—Entwine, enfold.

Caresses.—Acts of endearment, chiefly embraces. Gr. Katarezzo.

65–66. **Wantoning.**—Disporting, revelling. This whole picture always reminds me of Murillo's " Our Lady of the Apocalypse," more generally known as the " Immaculate Conception." It is a revel of angels, about the feet of the great Lady-Mother.

Lady-Mother.—i. e., Nature.

Vagrant.—Latin, " vagare "—to stray, to wander. It gives the idea of tresses, curls, straying upon the cheek or brow, fresh and fair, with a happy, careless way of becoming untidy. It is an expressive word, and richly bears out the idea contained in *wantoning.*

Tresses.—Ringlets. Some derive the word from the Greek " trissos," threefold, as a tress is usually formed by interlacing three pieces.

67. **Banqueting.**—Feasting uproariously, yet most refinedly.

68–69. **Wind-walled palace** and **azured dais** both have reference to the open skies where the revels of Nature are held.

Wind-walled.—The Palace of the Skies has no limit save the winds that blow.

Azured.—Colored blue, the color of the skies, " bleu céleste," called by painters. Azure is a blue pigment consisting of glass, fused with oxide of cobalt and ground to powder.

Dais.—Originally a raised platform at the end of a hall for the table of honor. Then it came to mean the table itself, and without losing either signification, is employed also (as here) in the sense of a canopy (over an altar or throne). The " s " is soft in the pronunciation.

70–79.
Quaffing, as your taintless way is,
From a chalice

Lucent-weeping out of the dayspring."
So it was done
I, in their delicate fellowship was one—
Drew the bolt of Nature's secrecies.
I knew all the swift importings
On the wilful face of skies;
I knew how the clouds arise,
Spumèd of the wild sea-snortings;

70. **Quaffing.**—Drinking copiously, in long draughts. A good old English word.

Taintless way.—Dainty fashion. Cf. Goldsmith (Deserted Village):

"And the coy maid half willing to be prest,
Shall kiss the cup to pass it to the next."

71. **Chalice.**—Cup, usually of some rich material. We say "chalice" of a flower, in Botany, "calyx."

72. **Lucent-weeping.**—Lucent, from the Latin, "lucere"—to shine. *Lucent-weeping*, therefore, conveys the idea of dripping and overflowing with light (they drink the sunshine,—it is a pretty figure) after having been steeped and filled in the *dayspring.*

Dayspring.—The fountain of light, the sun or the dawn. Cf. Job, xxxviii–12 (Protestant version): "Hast thou commanded the morning since the days and caused the dayspring (Vulgate—"the dawning of the day") to know his place?"

73–74. He is become one of them, a happy, careless child of Nature.

75. **Drew the bolt of Nature's secrecies.**—This was his mistake. All who draw this bolt too often or too much, or nearly all, fail to reach God, (of course, the poet's wish was to escape from Him) because they fail to "look thro' nature up to nature's God." (Pope—"Essay on Man"), God keeps the secret of Himself well,—He will not be questioned as to how and why. He just reveals to His "little ones." The Psalmist seems to think so (Psalm 70): "Because I have

not known learning (literaturam—literature?), I will enter into the powers (secrecies, secrets) of the Lord;" and a Kempis (Book I): "If thou didst know the whole Bible outwardly, and the sayings of all the philosophers, what would it all profit thee without charity and the grace of God."

76. **Swift importings.**—The frequent different manifestations,—the lights and shades.

77. **Wilful.**—Capricious, changeful.

Face of skies.—Cf. Line 95: *Heaven's grey cheek.*

79. **Spumed.**—Cast up, as foam or froth. Cf. fume.

80–86. All that's born or dies
Rose and drooped with; made them shapers
Of mine own moods, or wailful or divine—
With them joyed and was bereaven.
I was heavy with the even,
When she lit her glimmering tapers
Round the day's dead sanctities.

80–81. That is, "I rose and drooped with all that rose and drooped;"—he learned the secrets of life and death, the mysteries of Nature.

81–82. **Made Them shapers . . . . divine.**—His own moods took on the color of the expression of Nature. Hood, in his "Ode to Melancholy," says:

"Come let us sit and watch the sky,
And fancy clouds where no clouds be."

Children amuse themselves with fancies in the glowing embers in the fire-grate; "Faces in the fire" is my own earliest recollection.

Wailful.—Sorrowful; is a poor antithesis to the word *divine*, in its literal sense. By *divine*, is meant, of course, the higher feelings which we experience at times, each of us, on those rare days when we feel it is good to be alive, and would hate to die.

83. **Joyed.**—To rejoice, be glad. Cf. Hab. iii (Protestant version): "I will joy in the God of my salvation."

85–86. **A beautiful simile.**—Night, in the silence of her sorrow, lighting the glimmering tapers of the stars around the bier of a dead day, the sanctuary of a light and of a love departed. Thompson was a Catholic, and this custom of the 'chapelle ardente' was familiar to him.

85. **Lit** for lighted, is obsolete or colloquial.

Glimmering tapers.—Cf. Robert Buchanan (Book of Orm—of the stars):

"Ah! the lamps numberless,
The mystical jewels of God,
The luminous, wonderful,
Beautiful Lights of the Veil!"

86. **Day's dead sanctities.**—Like so many of Thompson's expressions, this is one of which we feel, rather than perceive, the meaning. *Sanctities* could mean sanctuary or the relics of the departed day—relics are holy.

87–95.
I laughed in the morning's eyes.
I triumphed and I saddened with all weather,
Heaven and I wept together,
And its sweet tears were salt with mortal mine;
Against the red throb of its sunset-heart
I laid my own to beat,
And share commingling heat;
But not by that, by that, was eased my human smart.
In vain my tears were wet on Heaven's grey cheek.

87. Smile kindling smile, and joy, joy.

88–89. It is the privilege and pain of all highly strung people to be influenced by the changes of the weather. Anything that bores or is tiresome is proverbially said to be as "long as a wet Sunday."

90. **Sweet tears.**—The tears of heaven, the rain-drops, have no cause to be bitter. Our tears are salt in the natural physical sense, and bitter in the sense that they usually spring from some painful emotion.

Mortal.—Deadly, painful, bitter.

91–95. The glowing heart of heaven has not the responsive human heart throb which human love demands; therefore, to *share commingling heat* and be consoled, was literally impossible; for the same reason, his tears fell idly upon the cold, grey unresponsive cheek of heaven.

Red.—Applying to *throb*, is an example of transferred epithet, as it really applies to *sunset-heart.*

Sunset heart.—Strange combination of words, and though the meaning is evident and quite natural, it is one of those expressions which only poets find.

My own.—i. e., my own heart.

Commingling heat.—*Share* is like *to beat,* infinitive mood, having *my own* (heart) for subject. He was longing for a heart-to-heart intercourse with Nature. Anything but God!

Smart.—A quick, pungent, lively pain.

Were wet.—Again the transferred epithet, because it is the *grey cheek* of Heaven which was wet.

Grey.—The dullest of colors—nothing warm about it. Nevertheless, like everything God has made, it has its own perfection and charm. Cf. the grey dawn, or the grey twilight,—but grey skies are sad.

96–104. For ah! we know not what each other says,
These things and I; in sound *I* speak—
Their sound is but their stir, they speak in silences.
Nature, poor stepdame, cannot slake my drouth;
Let her, if she would owe me,
Drop yon blue bosom-veil of sky, and show me
The breasts o' her tenderness:
Never did any milk of hers once bless
My thirsting mouth.

96–97. Thompson blames the heavens for unresponsiveness, but he was seeking from them what they could not give. To ask too much, even of a friend, is dangerous to friendship. But the soul that is closed to God will never find any answer in Nature, for Nature is God's mirror. Cf. Wordsworth (Peter Bell):

> " A primrose by a river's brim
> A yellow primrose was to him,
> And it was nothing more."

98. **Silences.**—The silences of which he complains are, nevertheless, filled with God. Byron, who loved God so very little, was impressed by them,—(Childe Harold):

> " There is a pleasure in the pathless woods,
> There is a rapture on the lonely shore,
> There is society, where none intrudes,
> By the deep sea, and music in its roar."

99. **Stepdame.**—He is tired of her, and so, pities her. Why is the adjective "poor" used to express pity? It is found in all languages. Stepmothers are proverbially hard-hearted and unkind.

Slake.—Slacken, allay.

Drouth.—Thirst, (akin to drink, draught). One of the prettiest things in the history of art is the prayer of Palestrina for his nephew, that God would grant him the sacred hunger for the ideal. It was Palestrina's own pain that he could never give, in even his music, the full sense or sentiment of the ideal harmonies that haunted his mind. They were too filled with God for human expression. Alas! for all our ideals!

100. **Owe me.**—Own me, claim me as her child or her slave.

101–102. The sky was formerly Mother Nature's canopy; now, it is wound around her as a garment. Only to poets is this license permitted. The expression is pretty.

103–104. He was disappointed from the beginning, and this was his sin;—he knew he would be. Wordsworth, the great lover of Nature, came to a different conclusion (Tintern Abbey):

"Nature never did betray
The heart that loved her."

105–111. Nigh and nigh draws the chase,
With unperturbèd pace,
Deliberate speed, majestic instancy,
And past those noisèd Feet
A Voice comes yet more fleet—
"Lo! naught contents thee, who content'st not Me."
Naked I wait Thy Love's uplifted stroke!

105–110. **Nigh and nigh.**—Nearer and nearer come the Feet of God. "Chaser" would be logically more correct here. Although Nature did not console or shelter him, nevertheless, she brought him nearer to God, for the Voice "*more fleet*" has now passed ahead of the ring of the Feet, and is calling out to him, what he was hiding from himself, namely, that it is contentment he is seeking, not shelter from God.

110. It is an echo of the famous aspiration of St. Augustin (Confessions): "Thou hast made us for Thyself, O Lord, and our heart is forever unrested, until it rest in Thee."

111. Now, indeed, he has tempted all God's servitors, but in vain! He is on the cross; will he, or will he not, accept? He is face to face with what the "Imitation of Christ" says no one can escape: "The Cross of Christ." A reviewer of the poem in the "Bookman," struck the keynote of criticism when he said: "It is the return of the nineteenth century to Thomas a Kempis." Cf. Imitation, Book II, Ch. 12.

Naked.—Deprived of everything, even of hope. This is the climax of the poem.

I wait.—Await. Some years ago, an active and rather acrid discussion was carried on, as to the relative merits of the active and passive virtues. It is the old question of Martha and Mary. Both were saints, but Mary, the passive, chose "the better part." The sooner we put ourselves completely in God's hands, the better, doing at the same time all we can to co-operate with His graces.

Thy.—This is the first time he speaks to God in the second person.

Love's uplifted stroke.—It is much to acknowledge even that it is God's love which causes us to suffer.

112–123. My harness piece by piece Thou hast hewn from me,
And smitten me to my knee;
I am defenceless utterly.
I slept, methinks, and woke,
And, slowly gazing, find me stripped in sleep.
In the rash lustihead of my young powers,
I shook the pillaring hours
And pulled my life upon me; grimed with smears,
I stand amid the dust o' the mounded years—
My mangled youth lies dead beneath the heap.
My days have crackled and gone up in smoke,
Have puffed and burst as sun-starts on a stream.

112. **Harness.**—A word found in old romances, meaning armor. (It is much more prosaic now in signification, meaning the collection of articles used for yoking animals to wagons.) Tennyson (Morte d'Arthur) "Dry clash'd his harness in the icy caves."

Piece by piece.—The knights' armour was composed of several pieces, notably the shield, helmet, breastplate, gauntlets, and greaves. This necessitated an esquire or armour-bearer, who attended the knight, and carried his fighting equipment which he buckled on his master before the combat.

Hewn.—Hacked away, as if with a sword.

113. **Smitten.**—Past participle of "to smite"—to strike. Cf. Tennyson (Morte d'Arthur): ". . . . smitten thro' the helm."

To my knee.—Position of defeat, as well as of supplication.

114. **I am defenceless utterly.**—He is now very near to

God, without Whom we can do absolutely nothing. This is a terrible revelation to some souls, (for we are all Pelagians at heart, and would wish to be able to work out our salvation without God's grace)—the fact that with all their striving, they get no closer to God, for they hit wide of the mark all the time by not preparing for and awaiting God's coming to them. What we can and must do is to co-operate with God's grace.

115. The awakening from the dream of his life. It seems to him that heretofore his life was but a dream, and now he realizes it.

116–123. All this passage is a parallel to the incident related of Samson in the Book of Judges, Chapter XVI. Samson's strength was in his hair, and while he was sleeping, he was shorn of his hair, and so of his strength, by Delilah. (The poet, too, was stripped in sleep, and awoke ***defenceless utterly.***) Samson was then taken prisoner by his old enemies, the Philistines, and his eyes were plucked out. (The poet, too, on his awakening found himself ***slowly gazing*** like a blind man.) Samson was finally brought one day into the temple of the Philistine god, Dagon, to be mocked. Calling on God for strength, he laid hands on the pillars supporting the building, and, shaking them, he pulled the temple in ruins, both on the Philistines and on himself. (So, too, with one great effort,—perhaps it was the effect of prayer,—in his address to God, ***Naked, I wait Thy Love's uplifted stroke,*** the poet shook the supports of the temple he had built for himself of his hopes and longings, and brought it down in ruins about him.)

117. **Lustihead.**—Lustihead, vigour of body, headstrong strength, energy.

Young powers.—Freshly recovered strength.

118. **Pillaring hours.**—See Line 2, *arches of years.*

119. **Pulled my life upon me.**—The ruin of the temple.

Grimed.—Begrimed, smeared.

Smears.—Stains, usually caused by some viscous substance.

120. **I stand.**—Can you imagine a ruin more complete?
Mounded.—Heaped up.

120–123. These lines are a fitting conclusion to this passage. They have all the lyricism of Hebrew poetry about them. Each line expresses the same idea, the complete ruin of the fabric of his life, with a parallelism that is distinctively the trait of the poetry of the East. Cf. Psalm ci:

V. 4.—For my days are vanished like smoke; and my bones are grown dry like fuel for the fire.

V. 5.—I am smitten as grass, and my heart is withered . . . . .

V. 6.—Through the voice of my groaning, my bone hath cleaved to my flesh.

V. 7.—I am become like to a pelican . . . a night-raven, ... a sparrow all alone, etc.

But Thompson's lines have a newness about them which almost makes us forget what the Psalmist felt and sang so long before him. They come "from the depth of some divine despair."

123. **Puffed and burst.**—How often have we seen this, and would have wished to express it so!

Sun-starts.—Flashes of sunlight on the water, through the overhanging trees.

124–125. **Yea, faileth now even dream**
The dreamer, and the lute the lutanist;

124–125. He is at length wide-awake, face to face with the reality of God's love.

Lute.—A musical instrument of the guitar kind, resembling in shape the horizontal section of a large pear, with a back like a mandolin; much used in the 16th and 17th centuries. Tradition associates it with love-songs, dream-songs. Cf. Vivien's song to Merlin in Tennyson's "Idylls of the King":

"'In Love, if Love be Love, if Love be ours,
. . . .
Unfaith in aught is want of faith in all.

It is the little rift within the lute,
That bye and bye will make the music mute.

. . . .

And trust me not at all or all in all.' "

What the lute is doing in this particular connection, I can scarcely say, except it be that the stern reality forces him to think he can no longer sing.

126–130. These lines pursue the same thought.

Linked phantasies—blossomy twist.—Convey the same idea, only reversed: "*Phantasies* (*fancies*) *blossomy; linked* and *twist* both refer to his song. He can no longer sing or rhapsodize for, as he states, the poetical fancies by which, as if by strings of flowers, he bound all things to him, are now yielding.

Trinket at my wrist.—The word "trinket" is of uncertain origin, but in our language it has come to mean a small ornament, particularly of Goldsmith's work. Strong in his imagination, he thought he was lord of the earth. But, now, that dream has gone. In the Greek Mythology, Europa held Jupiter (in the form of a white bull) very fast, and guided him thro' the meadows by means of a string of flowers. But the story tells how he finally dashed into the sea, and swam away with her. She trusted too much to the *blossomy twist.* And, indeed, in all our loves, we are bound only by a fragile string of flowers, as it were, which one day will go to pieces. We are "bound with gold chains about the feet of God," alone. Thompson tried to break these chains, and he failed.

Yielding.—Giving way.

Cords of all too weak account.—Of too little strength entirely to be taken into account.

Heavy griefs.—Sorrow is the principal element in our lives which disentangles us from the earth, and the earth is, indeed, heavy with it.

Overplussed.—Verb formed from noun "overplus"—excess.

131–140. Ah! is Thy love indeed
A weed, albeit an amaranthine weed,
Suffering no flowers except its own to mount?
Ah! must—
Designer infinite!—
Ah! must Thou char the wood ere Thou canst limn with it?
My freshness spent its wavering shower i' the dust;
And now my heart is as a broken fount,
Wherein tear-drippings stagnate, spilt down ever
From the dank thoughts that shiver
Upon the sighful branches of my mind.

130–132. This is his first genuine thought of God, and it is a bitter one. He is beginning to reflect. He calls God's love by the ugly name of *weed.* Weeds, as a matter of fact, choke up all other vegetation, and the strongest crowd out the weakest. "Ill weeds grow apace."

Albeit.—Although. Cf. so be it.

Amaranthine.—Adjective derived from "amaranth" (Gr. undecaying) a plant, or rather a genus of plants of several species. In poetry it is always understood as an imaginary flower, which never fades, i. e., it retains its color (purple) for a long time. Cowper writes:

"The only amaranthine flower on earth
Is virtue; the only lasting treasure, truth."
(The Garden)

Tennyson, in "The Lotos-eaters," sets this flower among those which surround the throne of the couch of the dreamers.

Suffering no other flowers . . . . . mount.—This is no revelation to him, only he tried to forget it, because he has already stated (lines 22, 23)—

"But, if one little casement parted wide,
The gust of His approach would clash it to."

133–135. The great secret of our relations with God is that Christ came to save the world, but He came to save it with the Cross and that, consequently, as St. Paul states it, "we must resemble the image of the Son." The process is a bitter one for human nature, and it is sometimes as painful as burning,—the rooting out of our nature all that is contrary to God, before God can make use of us for ourselves, for others, or for Himself.

Designer infinite.—Cf. The Great Architect of the Masons.

Char.—Burn. Charcoal is used by painters to draw the outlines of their subjects on the canvas.

Ere.—Before.

Limn.—Latin, "illuminare"—to draw or sketch.

136–140. Another much involved passage, although the meaning is almost evident. He compares his heart to a fountain, which spent its freshness in the dust and dross of things which are not God. It is grown old and broken, a receptacle only for occasional drops from the overhanging leaves.

137. **My heart is as a broken fount.**—There is a pathos about this line even deeper than in line 114—*defenceless utterly*—because the agony is no longer from without, but from within,—*a broken fount.* Ruins are always sad.

138–147. Wherein tear-drippings stagnate, spilt down ever
From the dank thoughts that shiver
Upon the sighful branches of my mind.
Such is; what is to be?
The pulp so bitter, how shall taste the rind?
I dimly guess what Time in mists confounds;
Yet ever and anon a trumpet sounds
From the hid battlements of eternity:
Those shaken mists a space unsettle, then
Round the half-glimpsed turrets slowly wash again;

138. **Tear-drippings stagnate.**—Because these are the useless tears, put to no purpose, and so they stagnate, growing more rank and bitter.

139–140. These two lines in my estimation are the weakest in the poem. The metaphor is too bold; and yet, they complete the picture of desolation and ruin.

139. **Dank.**—Moist, clammy. Washington Irving, in his "Sketch Book," speaking of English scenery, mentions urns "grown green and dank with age," mildewed. *Dank thoughts* is certainly a far-fetched expression.

140. **Sighful.**—Full of sighs, sad, lonely.

Branches of my mind.—The metaphor is too bold; yet, it is picturesque and expressive. I have seen in the old churchyards of Ireland ruins of churches all covered with ivy, and have imagined how lonely it must be to hear the winds sighing there at night.

141. Is this the recklessness of hope or of despair?

142. **Pulp—rind.**—Cf. of a fruit. He has tasted of the pulp and found it bitter. Is the rind God?

143. Eternity is drawing closer. Time is but its dawn, the misty dawn.

144–147. These lines remind me of another famous picture: Romney's "Piel Castle" (in a storm). But the beauty of Thompson's lines is all his own. It is the trumpet-call, the summons from the castle-walls, before the drawbridge is let down, so familiar to any reader of Sir Walter Scott. But the ramparts are here those of eternity. The blast of the trumpet shakes the mists apart, the mists in which time confounds everything, and a fleeting glimpse is caught of the towers and parapets of eternity before the mists wash back again. The whole thing is gorgeous in its imagery. One has only to shut one's eyes to see and hear it all. The drawbridge will soon be let down, and the poor worn-out stranger will be welcomed to the Heart of the Lord of lords and King of kings.

144. **Ever and anon.**—Now and again. Anon means quickly, soon. The Americans say "Once in a while."

145. **Battlements.**—Originally constructed for defense; now used only as ornaments in architecture.

147. **Wash.**—A very expressive word used, of course, not in the active sense. Trailing mist clouds are often seen along the sides of mountains, and can be easily imagined in this picture. Tennyson (Morte d'Arthur) makes use of the word "wash" in this sense:

"'I heard the water lapping on the crag,
And the long ripple washing in the reeds.'"

And we say "back-wash" of a wave.

148–154. But not ere him who summoneth
I first have seen, enwound
With glooming robes purpureal, cypress-crowned;
His name I know, and what his trumpet saith.
Whether man's heart or life it be which yields
Thee harvest, must Thy harvest fields
Be dunged with rotten death?

148–150. He catches his first glimpse of God, and God looks terrible to him.

149. **Enwound.**—Clothed, garbed, encased in.

150. **Glooming robes purpureal.**—Dark, but they have the royal color, purple, purpureal. Note the majesty expressed in this line.

Cypress-crowned.—Wearing a crown of cypress leaves. Cypresses are distinguished from firs and pines by their leaves being mere scales, miniature ramifications. These leaves are easily woven into a crown, owing to their shape. The cypress is usually connected in our minds with death and cemeteries, but the reason is that on account of its ever-greenness, it is a symbol, not of death, but of immortality. And God is immortal.

151. **His name I know.**—God gave His Name to Moses—"I am Who am," and philosophy teaches that God is exactly that, identically the same in essence and existence.

152–154. **What His trumpet saith.**—The message, which is the message of Christ to the world.

152–154. This is the message. John xii–24, 25; "Amen,

amen, I say to you, unless the grain of wheat falling into the ground, die, itself remaineth alone. But if it die, it bringeth forth much fruit. He that loveth his life shall lose it, and he that hateth his life in this world, keepeth it unto life eternal." Now, life springs from the seed, but alas! the seed must first rot and die. It is a universal law in nature, summed up by St. Thomas: "Corruptio unius, generatio alterius,"—"corruption and generation are simultaneous." It is so, too, in the ways God has with our souls and our lives. If ever God is to reap a harvest from us, it will be only if the harvest field is dunged with the dead bodies of our own achievements. God builds upon nothing and nothingness, just as He created from nothing and nothingness.

154. **Death.**—Dead things.

155–176.
Now of that long pursuit
Comes on at hand the bruit;
That Voice is round me like a bursting sea:
"And is thy earth so marred,
Shattered in shard on shard?
Lo, all things fly thee, for thou fliest Me!
Strange, piteous, futile thing!
Wherefore, should any set thee love apart?
Seeing none but I makes much of naught" (He said)
"And human love needs human meriting:
How hast thou merited—
Of all man's clotted clay the dingiest clot?
Alack, thou knowest not
How little worthy of any love thou art!
Whom wilt thou find to love ignoble thee,
Save Me, save only Me?
All which I took from thee I did but take,
Not for thy harms,
But just that thou might'st seek it in My arms.
All which thy child's mistake
Fancies as lost, I have stored for thee at home:
Rise, clasp My hand, and come."

155. The chase is drawing to a close.

156. **Bruit.**—Indistinct noise, report, rumor; French, "bruit" rarely used in English.

157. **Bursting sea.**—Cf. Tennyson (Crossing the Bar):

"But such a tide as moving seems asleep,
Too full for sound and foam."

That is, full to bursting.

158–176. What the Voice of God says explaining—

(*a*) The *external* causes of our sufferings (in lines 158–160), namely, we put our confidence in things outside of us, which are not God, and suffer when we are deprived of them.

(*b*) The *internal* cause of our sufferings (in lines 161–170), namely our need of love and our unworthiness of any love, despite which we, nevertheless, expect to be loved. Oscar Wilde in "De Profundis," came to the conclusion that no one deserves to be loved except the one who counts himself unworthy of all love; and furthermore, he beautifully says that the wonderful thing about God's love is that it is "eternally given to that which is eternally unworthy."

(*c*) The *final* cause, (i. e., the reason why we suffer) of our sufferings (in lines 171–176), namely, that God permits us to suffer externally and internally *that we may seek Him*, and our happiness in Him.

158. **Marred.**—Disfigured, ruined, shattered, wrecked.

159. **Shard on shard.**—Shard is broken pottery; cf. Potsherd. There is a hillock on the banks of the Tiber, near Rome, called Monte Testaccio (Latin, "testa,"—an earthenware pot or jug. Horace addresses, in the Odes, his wine-jar as "pia-testa"—"loving-cup") formed entirely from pieces of broken pottery. I understand it was on this spot that the boats unloaded grain which they brought in earthenware receptacles. I submit this observation to show that the poet's simile is not as far-fetched as it might seem. Besides, human life and human hopes have been often compared, on account of their fragility, to clay vessels. It is

frequent in the Bible. Omar Khayyam in his "Rubayiat" would have us nothing else than such clay vessels, some beautifully and some villainously formed by the Potter. As for himself, he states that he "was never deep in anything but—wine." It is the most pagan of poems. I prefer that little song of Longfellow's, "Turn, turn, my wheel," inserted in his poem "Keramos"—it is Christian. In it we find:

"These vessels made of clay.
. . . .
Behind us in our path we cast
The broken potsherds of the past."

160. This is the return to the "Imitation of Christ" (Book I, Ch. I): "Vanity of vanities, and all is vanity, but to love God and serve Him alone."

161. **Strange, piteous, futile.**—Words full of tender commiseration. *Strange*—in thought, desire and action; *piteous*—pitiable for so many "child's mistakes;" *futile*—of no account in all its efforts, for "without Me you can do nothing."

Thing.—A word so full of pity; it is the climax of the line.

162–168. Why should anyone ever love us? When we love anyone, it is not so much the object of our love whom we love, as that very person *as he seems to us.* Our own loving imagination makes him lovable, and love is an act of the will. That is why human love, purely human love, is generally so selfish, because our love for others is thus only a modification of our love for ourselves. And besides, that is why so many are disappointed. A day comes when the dear object of our love and affection stands revealed in all its weakness and native vileness,—he was *only clay,* and we did not know it,—and that is the day of disillusionment and disenchantment. Love, therefore, that is only human—from man to man—is the adoration of the idol of clay. "Why, then," indeed, "should any set thee love apart?"

163. Too true! The world does not take naught into account. But, strange to say, God does. St. Paul found it out long ago (I Cor. 1–27, 28): "But the foolish things of the world hath God chosen, that He may confound the wise. And the weak things of the world hath God chosen that He may confound the strong. And the base things of the world, and the things that are contemptible, hath God chosen and things that are not, that He might bring to naught the things that are. . . ."

164. God's love alone is given freely. Cf. Lowell (Vision of Sir Launfal):

> "'T is heaven alone that is given away,
> 'T is only God may be had for the asking."

165. **How hast thou merited.**—Thou art no greater, no better than thy fellows, since "every heart is human, and made of the same clay."

166. **Clotted clay.**—Puddled earth.

Dingiest.—Dingy means dusky, brownish—here, of course, soiled and soiling.

167–168. This is the "last straw" in the close reasoning of God: our great unworthiness. It falls on the soul from the lips of God like a machine hammer, reducing what is left of the miserable being to powder, to clay!

Alack.—Alas; cf. lack-a-day.

169–170. If Thompson had written nothing more than these two lines, he would have merited our gratitude forever. Whom, indeed, could we ever find to love us, if all were known and said, and done, except God, except our *good, good God!* "Save *Me*, save only *Me!*" These are God-like words.

171–173. THE REVELATION: God deprives the soul of everything so that the soul may go to Him for everything.

172. **Not for thy harms.**—Not to hurt or harm thee, not for the sake of making thee suffer. And this is why suffering is the true mark of God's chosen souls: His love for us causes Him to make us suffer,—and how badly we understand His love!

173–End. But just that thou might'st seek it in My arms.
All which thy child's mistake
Fancies as lost, I have stored for thee at home:
Rise, clasp My hand, and come."

Halts by me that footfall;
Is my gloom, after all,
Shade of His hand, outstretched caressingly?
"Ah, fondest, blindest, weakest,
I am He whom thou seekest!
Thou dravest love from thee, who dravest Me."

173–175. THE CONSOLATION. We seek God because we are made for Him alone, even in our sins because we seek "good" when we sin, and God is the Supreme "Good." The mistake we make—God calls it a *child's mistake*—but it is a terrible one (and a child would not make it)—is to seek God where God is not, and can never be. And when the "good" we seek, even in our sins, leaves us and betrays us, God will tell us that if we turn to Him, we shall find all we sought and sought in vain, stored for us at home, with Him in Heaven, in His arms.

176. **Rise, clasp My hand, and come.**—It is the invitation in the beautiful second chapter of the Canticle of Canticles, v. 13: "Arise, my love, my beautiful one, and come." It is the life of all the saints, in one line: to arise from the earth, clasp God's hand tight, and walk forever hand in hand with Him. Happy those who heed God's invitation!

177. **Halts by me that footfall.**—The race is over and God has won. . . . . . It is the peace of God, the peace which the world cannot know or give.

178–179. All our sorrows are, indeed, if we only knew,—once again our *child's mistake,*—the shadow of God's hand stretched out to bless, and—to caress.

180–182. These lines sound like the echoing of the "Lost Chord" of Adelaide Proctor: "The sound of a great Amen!"

Fondest.—Fond originally meant foolish.

181. THE CONSOLATION. No blame for the straying one, only ineffable tenderness, and a great welcome. "Come to Me, all you who labor and are heavily laden, and I will refresh you."

182. And this is the last word of everything:

GOD IS LOVE.—
Thank God that it is so!